PLANET FOOTBALL

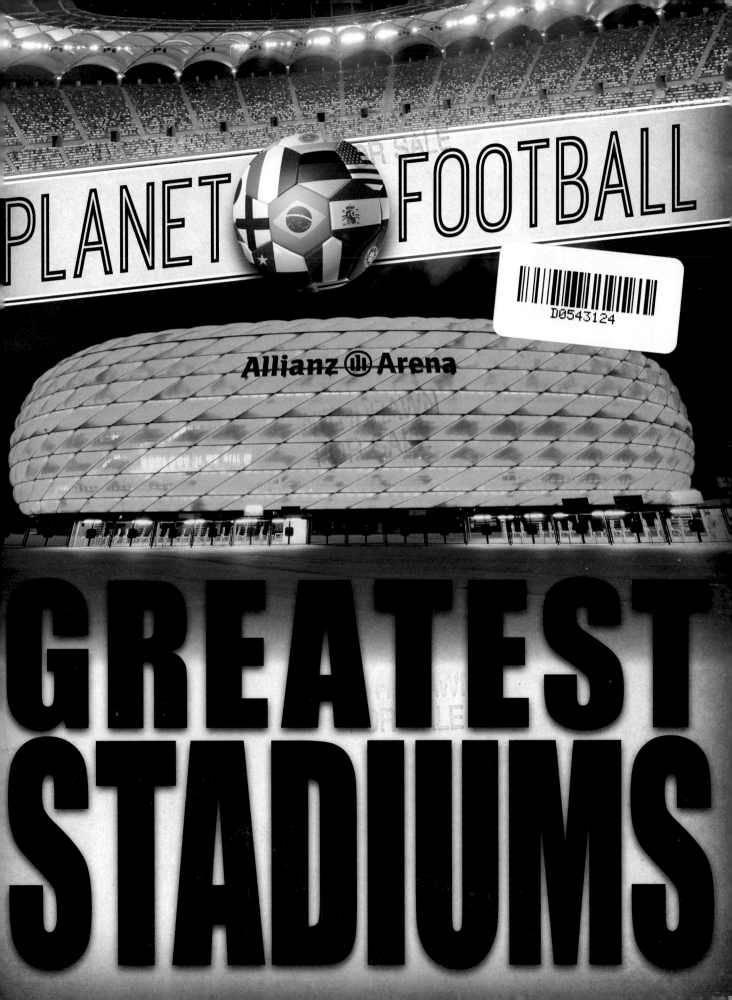

Allianz (ᴜ) Arena

GREATEST STADIUMS

CONTENTS

Published in paperback in 2017
Copyright © Hodder and
Stoughton, 2017
All rights reserved

Editor: Victoria Brooker
Produced for Wayland by
Tall Tree Ltd
Designer: Gary Hyde
Editor: Jon Richards

Dewey number: 796.3'34'068-
dc23
ISBN 978 1 5263 0345 5

Wayland, an imprint of
Hachette Children's Group
Part of Hodder and Stoughton
Carmelite House
50 Victoria Embankment
London EC4Y 0DZ
An Hachette UK Company
www.hachette.co.uk
www.hachettechildrens.co.uk

FSC
Printed and bound in China
10 9 8 7 6 5 4 3 2 1

CATHEDRALS OF FOOTBALL

A football ground or stadium is more than just a pitch and somewhere to view the game. For some fans, it's a home from home. It's where they go to see their side play, meet and mingle with their fellow fans beforehand and enjoy the big match atmosphere.

STADIUM DONBAS

THE YELLOW WALL

One of the most notable standing sections is the Yellow Wall of the Signal Iduna Park – the home ground of German club, Borussia Dortmund. This giant stand runs the length of the pitch and can hold 25,000 people.

The first dedicated football grounds were built in England in the 1860s and 1870s. Some still survive, such as Bramall Lane in Sheffield and Deepdale in Preston. Thousands of new grounds have since been built all over the world. They have become places that are dearly loved by fans.

Fans head towards the Melbourne Rectangular Stadium during the AFC Asian Cup in 2015. The 30,000-capacity stadium hosted seven matches during the tournament which saw the hosts, Australia, become champions for the first time.

In the past, many stadiums had few seats and most fans at football grounds stood to watch the game on open terraces or stands with roofs. Today, many of the world's biggest and best grounds are all-seater stadiums. However, some, particularly in Germany but also in Sweden, Belgium and Uruguay, still have standing sections.

RECTANGULAR

NUMBERS GAME

1,365,050

The number of fans that watched the 17 Bundesliga matches at the Signal Iduna Park in 2013/14, an average of 80,297 per game and the highest in the world.

Opened in 2009 with a concert by Beyoncé, the Stadium Donbas in Ukraine hosted games during Euro 2012 and is used as a club stadium by Shakhtar Donetsk. The stadium holds over 52,000 spectators.

"THE THOUSANDS WHO COME HERE, COME TO WORSHIP... IT'S A SORT OF SHRINE, IT ISN'T A FOOTBALL GROUND."
BILL SHANKLY, LEGENDARY LIVERPOOL FC MANAGER

GREAT GROUNDS OF EUROPE

Football expanded from the UK to Europe before spreading all over the world. Europe remains the centre of many of the world's biggest leagues and football clubs and boasts lots of amazing club stadiums.

New stadiums in Europe are springing up all the time. When Portugal hosted Euro 2004, seven new stadiums were built including the Estádio da Luz. In Italy, almost all of the biggest grounds are owned by local governments. In 2011, Juventus became the first top Italian club to own their ground when they moved to the new Juventus Stadium.

JUVENTUS

Juventus' opening game at their new stadium was against English club, Notts County, who back in 1903, sent them a set of black and white shirts which became Juventus' colours.

ESTÁDIO DA LUZ

Real Madrid have been champions of Europe ten times, more than any other club. Their home ground, the Bernabéu, opened in 1947. It has since hosted the final of a European Championship (1964) and a World Cup (1982) as well as four European Cup and Champions League finals.

NUMBERS GAME

12,000,000

The number of spectators that had watched matches at the Estádio da Luz by August, 2014.

BERNABÉU

The Santiago Bernabéu stadium was named after the club president and currently holds 85,454 spectators. There are plans to have that number increased to over 90,000 and a fully opening and closing roof added before 2020.

"I'VE BEEN FORTUNATE ENOUGH TO TAKE THE FIELD AT ANY NUMBER OF STADIUMS, BUT THE BERNABÉU REALLY TAKES YOUR BREATH AWAY."

NICOLAS ANELKA ON THE BERNABÉU

THEATRE OF DREAMS

Old Trafford was built in 1910, just eight years after the Newton Heath football club had changed its name to Manchester United. It has since developed into one of the most famous club grounds in Europe.

Old Trafford cost £60,000 to build, but during World War II, heavy bombing on the large industrial estates nearby saw much of the ground destroyed. Manchester United had to play at the Maine Road ground of their fierce rivals, Manchester City for eight years.

STRETFORD END ✚

The West Stand, known as the Stretford End, became all-seater in 1993. It was originally a standing terrace for more than 20,000 fans. Old Trafford was one of many grounds designed by the architect, Archibald Leitch, including Anfield (Liverpool) and Stamford Bridge (Chelsea).

The United Trinity statue stands outside Old Trafford's East Stand featuring three United legends, George Best, Dennis Law and Bobby Charlton. In 2012, a further statue was added outside the ground of United manager, Sir Alex Ferguson.

UNITED TRINITY

Old Trafford's first match in 1910 saw the home team lose 4-3 to Liverpool but the club went on to win the English league that season. In the 1990s onwards, Old Trafford was developed and extra seats added to bring the capacity up to 75,957, the biggest in England.

NUMBERS GAME

1,100,000

The number of fans who visit Old Trafford's Megastore per season. The shop offers more than 800 different Manchester United items.

WHARFSIDE WAY

"THIS IS MANCHESTER UNITED FOOTBALL CLUB, THIS IS THE THEATRE OF DREAMS."

SIR BOBBY CHARLTON, LEGENDARY MANCHESTER UNITED ATTACKER

THE CAMP NOU

Barcelona is one of the best known and exciting club teams in Europe and its ground is equally admired. It is the largest club stadium, not just in Spain but the whole of Europe, and can hold up to 99,354 fans.

Barcelona moved from their old ground, the Camp de Les Corts, to the Camp Nou in 1957. They immediately celebrated in style by notching up a 6-1 win over Jaen in their first Spanish league match there. The Camp Nou stands 48 m high and contains a large museum dedicated to the club and its players as well as a religious chapel next to the players' changing rooms.

MEMORABILIA

Exhibits from the Camp Nou Museum inside the stadium. In 2014, 1,530,484 football fans visited the museum, making it one of the most popular visitor attractions in northern Spain.

MES QUE UN CLUB

Over the years a series of gifted Barcelona sides have turned the Camp Nou into a footballing fortress. Barcelona proved very difficult to defeat on their home ground and were unbeaten at home in the Spanish league for 67 games in a row (1972–1976). In 2014, the club celebrated its 1,000th league game at the Camp Nou with a 3-0 win over Celta Vigo.

The Camp Nou's East Stand features seats in the club's colours including yellow seats that spell out Barcelona's official motto of, 'Mes Que Un Club' – More Than A Club.

"I KNOW HOW IT IS TO PLAY AT THE CAMP NOU – YOU HAVE TO KEEP YOUR MISTAKES TO A MINIMUM AND ONLY THEN CAN YOU SUCCEED."
PARIS ST GERMAIN STRIKER, ZLATAN IBRAHIMOVIC

THE SAN SIRO

Some stadiums are used by more than one football club. Careful timetabling is needed so that each club can play its home games at the stadium. One of the most famous ground shares occurs at the majestic Giuseppe Meazza Stadium, better known as the San Siro, in Milan, Italy.

AC Milan's dedicated fans group, known as ultras, form a colourful display during a Serie A match versus Juventus.

The San Siro is home to two of Italy's most famous and successful clubs – AC Milan and Internazionale (also known as Inter). Both teams have won Serie A (the Italian league) 18 times and are fierce rivals. Inter won their first derby match at the San Siro all the way back in 1926 and lead Milan with 77 wins to 74 out of 215 games.

AC MILAN V INTER

At its opening, the San Siro held 35,000 but was quickly built up to accommodate as many as 100,000 fans. Today, it is an all-seater stadium which can hold just over 80,000 and is considered one of the most famous football grounds in the world.

Inside the San Siro, spectators are shielded from the rain and snow by a large roof made of a steel frame covered with polycarbonate panels.

INSIDE THE SAN SIRO

There are 11 distinctive circular towers, each over 50 m high, around the outside of the San Siro. These support the giant roof and provide a long spiral walkway up to the highest seats.

"SOMETIMES, I HAVE THE ACTUAL FEELING THAT THE SAN SIRO IS MY SECOND HOME."
FORMER AC MILAN DEFENDER, PAULO MALDINI

GROUND MOVES

Many clubs find that they outgrow their old ground, or cannot repair it – so they look for a new one. Moving grounds can be upsetting for fans, but most find that their new stadium is bigger, brighter and packed with better facilities than before.

Many clubs move to accommodate more fans. Galatasaray is Turkey's most successful club yet until 2011 was playing at the Ali Sami Yen stadium which held less than 25,000 spectators. Their new ground, the Turk Telekom Arena, holds over double that, with a record 52,044 fans crammed in to watch the Turkish club play Spanish giants, Real Madrid in 2013.

NUMBERS GAME

131.76

The number of decibels the crowd in the Turk Telekom Arena reached in 2011. It set the record for the loudest crowd roar at a football stadium.

TURK TELEKOM ARENA

Since the Turk Telekom Arena ground opened, it has hosted Galatasaray's home matches as well as seven games played by the Turkish national team and matches of the 2013 Under-20 World Cup tournament.

60,000

The number of cubic metres of concrete used to build the Emirates Stadium – enough to fill the team bath at Arsenal's former stadium 7,500 times.

In 2006, English Premier League club Arsenal moved to the brand-new Emirates Stadium. Many fans missed their old ground, Highbury, where Arsenal had played for over 90 years. The new stadium, however, was less than a kilometre from Highbury.

Arsenal's Emirates Stadium in north London cost around £390 million pounds to build. The new stadium has a capacity of 60,272, which is 22,000 more than the capacity of the old Highbury ground.

BERGKAMP STATUE

The Emirate Stadium features giant murals of 32 Arsenal legends including Thierry Henry and Ian Wright. There are also statues of famous players including Dutch attacker, Denis Bergkamp (above).

"YOU CANNOT BE IN A BUSINESS WHERE YOU TURN DOWN 15,000 OR 20,000 PEOPLE EVERY WEEK."
ARSENAL MANAGER, ARSENE WENGER ON THE MOVE TO THE EMIRATES STADIUM

MUNICH ALLIANZ ARENA

Bayern Munich is Germany's most successful club. They have won the Bundesliga (German League) 25 times and the UEFA Champions League five times, so their stadium move was big news. It occurred in 2005 when they moved into the brand-new Allianz Arena, which they share with neighbours, TSV 1860 Munchen.

The outside of the stadium is covered in 2,760 diamond-shaped panels made of plastic. These can shine red, white or blue, depending on which home team is playing. On a clear night, the shining stadium can be seen as far away as the neighbouring country of Austria!

STADIUM EXTERIOR

The Allianz Arena's three tiers of seating originally held 66,000 fans and has already been extended to hold 71,000 with plans to add at least 4,000 more. Many fans make use of the stadium's enormous 9,800 berth car park – the biggest underground car park in Europe.

Since Roy Makaay scored the first competitive goal at the new ground in 2005, the stadium has been home to some impressive scoring feats. In 2015, Bayern thrashed Bundesliga rivals, Hamburg, 8-0 and shortly after, defeated Porto 6-1 in the Champions League. The stadium also hosted the 2012 UEFA Champions League final.

The Allianz Arena's pitch measures 105 x 68 and is made up of 320 tonnes of grass turf. Underneath the pitch, some 27 km of 3.2-cm diameter pipes carry hot water to provide undersoil heating.

Allianz (III) Arena

NUMBERS GAME

700,000

The number of German sausages eaten by fans inside the Allianz Arena in its first season (2005–06).

WORLD CUP WONDERS

The FIFA World Cup is the world's biggest football competition and its final is the biggest game in football. The host nation or nations modernise old stadiums, build new ones and devote their best and usually biggest stadium to the World Cup Final.

The Estadio Centenario today holds up to 76,609 fans and is used by the national team for their home games as well as Penarol, one of the leading clubs in Uruguay. It features a 100-m (330-ft) tall tower, built to commemorate 100 years since the country's independence in 1830.

The first World Cup final in 1930 was held at the Estadio Centenario in Uruguay's capital, Montevideo. The stadium was built in less than nine months and hosted 10 of the tournament's 18 games including the final in which the home nation became the first world champions, beating Argentina 4-2.

ESTADIO CENTENARIO

The FNB Stadium was known as Soccer City during the 2010 World Cup in which it hosted seven matches as well as the final between Spain and the Netherlands. The stadium also held three matches in the 2013 African Cup of Nations and is used by South African clubs such as the Kaizer Chiefs.

FNB STADIUM

The FNB Stadium was first built in 1989, close to the Soweto district of Johannesburg. In the lead up to the 2010 World Cup, the stadium got a major makeover. It was redesigned so that its outside looked like an African pot called a calabash, which became the ground's nickname.

NUMBERS GAME

94,736

The maximum capacity of the FNB Stadium, making it the largest football ground in Africa.

LUZHNIKI STADIUM

Work progresses on the Luzhniki Stadium in Moscow, Russia. The Luzhniki was built in the 1950s and has already hosted a UEFA Champions League final and the 1980 Olympics. It will host both the opening game and the final of the 2018 FIFA World Cup.

THE MARACANÃ

It was a race against time to finish Brazil's biggest stadium in time for the 1950 FIFA World Cup. The ground opened just eight days before holding the first game of the tournament. It was officially named the Estádio Jornalista Mário Filho but became known as the Maracanã, after a small river nearby.

WORLD CUP FINAL

The Maracanã hosted eight 1950 World Cup games including the final. After the World Cup, four clubs from Rio de Janeiro (Vasco da Gama, Botafogo, Flamengo and Fluminense) used it as their home ground. The world record attendance for a club match occurred when Flamengo played Fluminense in 1963 in front of 194,603 fans.

The stadium was reopened in 2013 with a friendly match between Brazil and England which ended 2-2. Its new fibreglass roof was fitted with 1,500 solar panels to generate electricity.

"THE MARACANÃ IS A SPECIAL PLACE FOR ALL BRAZILIANS... THE AURA OF THE PLACE IS EXTRAORDINARY."
FOOTBALL LEGEND PELÉ WHO SCORED HIS FIRST GOAL FOR BRAZIL AND HIS 1,000TH OF HIS CAREER AT THE MARACANÃ

The Maracanã got a makeover in time for Brazil's second World Cup in 2014. The lower tiers of the ground were completely redesigned and a new extended roof fitted to shield spectators from the weather. The Maracanã hosted seven 2014 FIFA World Cup games including the final between Germany and Argentina.

CHANGING ROOMS

NUMBERS GAME

333

The number of goals scored by Brazilian striker, Zico at the Maracanã, the most of any player.

Viewed from the air, the Maracanã appears as a giant oval ring in the Brazilian city of Rio de Janeiro. It originally held up to 200,000 people but now has a capacity of 78,838.

ESTADIO AZTECA

Mexico's greatest stadium is now the biggest football ground in the Americas. The Estadio Azteca took over four years to build and opened in 1966. It was the result of its architects travelling through Europe to see the continent's best stadiums.

Built for the 1968 Olympics and 1970 World Cup, the Azteca has three tiers of seats. These form a continuous ring around the pitch which is sunk 9.5m below ground level. At its peak it held over 115,000 but even reduced to 95,500, it remains a noisy and atmospheric ground when full.

EPIC GAMES

EL ESTADIO AZTECA, RINDE HOMENAJE A LAS SELECCIONES DE:

ITALIA (4) Y ALEMANIA (3)

PROTAGONISTAS EN EL MUNDIAL DE 1970, DEL

"PARTIDO DEL SIGLO"

17 DE JUNIO DE

A bronze plaque on the outside of the stadium records an epic semi-final match between Italy and Germany at the 1970 World Cup which Italy won 4-3.

After hosting ten games at the 1970 World Cup, the Azteca got a second chance to shine at the World Cup when planned hosts, Colombia were unable to hold the 1986 tournament and Mexico stepped in. The Azteca became the first ground to host the final match of two World Cups and also held the 1993 and 2003 CONCACAF Gold Cup competitions.

INTERIOR OF AZTECA

Fans get great views from all parts of the stadium as they watch a MX Liga match inside the Azteca. Club América play their home games at the stadium whilst other Mexican clubs including Nexaca and Club Azul have used the stadium in the past.

NUMBERS GAME

119,853

The Azteca's record attendance for a football match, in 1968, when the Mexico national team recorded a famous 2-1 win against Brazil.

EXTERIOR OF AZTECA

Estadio Azteca

Located in Mexico City, the Azteca needed 180,000 tonnes of rock removed for its base to be built below ground. The neighbouring black and red sculpture, 20.5 m tall, is called El Sol Rojo (the Red Sun) and was created by noted US sculptor, Alexander Calder.

"WE LOST THE 1986 (FIFA WORLD CUP) FINAL IN THE ESTADIO AZTECA WHICH, IN MY OPINION, IS THE MOST BEAUTIFUL STADIUM IN THE WORLD. I LOVE IT, SIMPLE AS THAT."
RUDI VOLLER, FORMER GERMAN ATTACKER

WEMBLEY STADIUM

In 1923, the Empire Stadium was opened in north London to host a huge exhibition featuring Britain and all its colonies. The stadium was to be demolished afterwards, but instead became Wembley Stadium – the home of the England national team.

In 2003, the original stadium was demolished. In its place, a brand new stadium was built featuring a retractable roof and a giant steel arch that stands 134 m tall. It holds up to 90,000 spectators who can buy food and drink at 688 different points around the ground.

OLD WEMBLEY

The twin towers of the original Wembley Stadium became a famous symbol of English football. The ground hosted the 1966 World Cup final which England won.

The first competitive game at the new ground saw the England and Italy Under 21 teams draw 3-3 and Italy's Giampaolo Pazzini became the first to score at the new ground, after just 28 seconds. The stadium hosted both the 2011 and 2013 UEFA Champions League final.

WEMBLEY SCREEN

One of the two giant screens that inform spectators at Wembley Stadium. Each is approximately the size of 600 home television screens.

Inside the stadium, there are three tiers of seats. Each of the seats has more legroom than the VIP seats at the original ground. If laid end to end, the rows of seats in the new Wembley would stretch 54 km.

"EVERY YOUNG CHILD WANTS TO PLAY AT WEMBLEY AND, FOR ME, IT'S THE ULTIMATE STADIUM... IT'S AN UNBELIEVABLE PLACE."
DAVID BECKHAM

STADIUM INNOVATIONS

Stadiums have evolved over the decades from stands made of wood and corrugated iron to today's venues, which not only often use advanced artificial materials but also increasingly offer cutting-edge technology inside the stadium.

Retractable roofs are often a feature of newly built stadiums. These can close so the stadium can hold indoor events but open for football matches. The Amsterdam ArenA, was the first football ground in Europe to feature a roof of this type. It weighs 520 tonnes (more than 100 monster trucks) and takes around 20 minutes to fully open or close.

SAPPORO DOME

The Sapporo Dome in Japan pioneered the use of roll-in pitches as the stadium hosts both baseball and football games. A complete grass football pitch is prepared elsewhere then brought into the stadium on a cushion of air, a little like a hovercraft. It allows the stadium to swap between sports surfaces in a matter of hours.

170 X 20

The size in metres of the giant LED screen fitted to the East stand of the Arena Corinthians Stadium in Brazil.

VIDEO CUBE

Big screens show replays and keep fans informed at some modern stadiums while other grounds, like Romania's National Arena (above), feature video cubes. These are four giant screens, often 30 m or more wide, placed in a square and suspended high above the middle of the pitch.

A number of grounds now feature some solar panels on the roof to generate a portion of the stadium's electricity. The large roof of the Stade de Suisse in the city of Bern generates a staggering 1.2 million kilowatt hours of electricity – enough to power the entire stadium and 400 houses nearby.

AMSTERDAM ARENA

The Amsterdam ArenA was built in the 1990s to provide a bigger home for Dutch club, Ajax, whose De Meer stadium only seated 19,000. The resulting ground boosted capacity to 53,052.

CRAZY STADIUMS

While many football stadiums look similar from a distance, some stand out due to their odd location or strange design. The Junguito Malucello stadium in Brazil, for example, has seats embedded in the earth of a hillside.

Some stadiums have been built in peculiar places. Croatia's Stadion Gospin Dolac is positioned right next to a 150-m drop into a lake, while the Eidi Stadium in the Faroe Islands is right on the coast, surrounded on two sides by the Atlantic Ocean. Singapore's Float Stadium is well-named as its pitch floats on the water.

THE FLOAT STADIUM

The Float is a floating football pitch moored to the seabed in Singapore's Marina Bay by six pylons. Stands on land provide seating for up to 30,000 people.

OLYMPIASTADION

NUMBERS GAME

200

The approximate number of metres apart that two Scottish stadiums – Tannadice Park (home of Dundee United) and Dens Park (home of Dundee) lie.

Munich's Olympiastadion was once Bayern Munich's ground and also hosted the 1974 World Cup final. Visitors can walk across its distinctive glass roof on a guided tour and descend to the ground on a climbing rope!

Portuguese club Braga's AXA Stadium was built in 2004. It was chiselled out of an old granite rock quarry and behind one goal is not rows of seats but a sheer rock face. Despite this strange arrangement, the ground holds up to 30,286 people and was used for the 2004 European Championships.

Braga's AXA Stadium required 15,000 tonnes of steel to be built. To move from one giant side stand to another, fans have to walk through an underground passage that runs directly beneath the pitch.

BRAGA STADIUM

A riot of colour, the Estadio Municipal de Aveiro in Portugal looks like it has been constructed out of giant toy bricks. Designed by Portuguese architect Tomás Taveira, the ground is the home of S.C. Beira-Mar and holds 30,200 fans.

AVIERO STADIUM

QUIZ

 1. The Maracanã stadium was built just in time for which football competition?

 2. Is Old Trafford, the Camp Nou or the Allianz Arena the biggest club ground in Europe?

3. What was the name of Arsenal's former ground before they moved to the Emirates Stadium?

4. The FNB Stadium is the largest football ground in which continent?

5. Which two Italian football clubs play at the San Siro stadium?

6. Was the Estadio Azteca, the Maracanã or the Camp Nou the first to host the final match of two World Cups?

7. In which country would you find a floating stadium?

8. Which club play at the first football ground in Europe to feature a retractable roof?

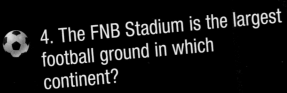
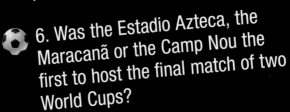

WEBSITES AND BOOKS

http://www.fifa.com/classicfootball/stadiums/
These webpages provide detailed descriptions and histories of some of the most memorable stadiums in world football.

http://www.worldstadiums.com/
The ultimate stadium database contains details of more than 10,000 grounds around the world, divided by continent and size.

http://www.premierleague.com/en-gb/clubs/stadium-tours/
Watch behind the scenes videos and 360 degree images of all the stadiums in the Premier League.

Truth or Busted: Football
by Adam Sutherland (Wayland, 2014)

Radar Top Jobs: Being a Professional Footballer
by Sarah Levete (Wayland, 2013)

Football Joke Book
by Clive Gifford (Wayland, 2013)

GLOSSARY

African Cup of Nations
A competition for the leading national teams of Africa held every two years.

architect
A person who designs buildings and other structures such as bridges and towers.

attendance
The number of people who watch a particular football match.

Bundesliga
The German league championship.

capacity
The maximum number of spectators that a stadium will seat.

CONCACAF
The organisation which runs football in North and Central America and the Caribbean. Its Gold Cup is its highest level competition for national teams from the region.

dressing room
The place in a stadium where the football team changes into its kit.

dugout
The area beside the pitch where a team's coaches and their substitutes sit during a game.

FIFA
Short for the *Fédération Internationale de Football Association*, the organisation that runs world football.

Liga MX
The top level league in Mexico containing 18 teams each season.

quarry
A place where rock and building materials can be dug from the ground.

retractable roof
A roof which can move back and forth to open or close.

solar panels
Special panels that convert sunlight into electricity.

UEFA Champions League
A competition for Europe's leading clubs held every year.

VIP
Short for very important person, such as country's leaders or heads of sports organisations that may attend matches.

ANSWERS

1. 1950 World Cup
2. Camp Nou
3. Highbury
4. Africa
5. AC Milan and Internazionale
6. Estadio Azteca
7. Singapore
8. Ajax

INDEX

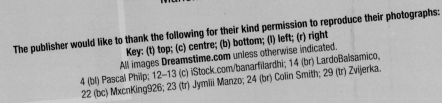

The publisher would like to thank the following for their kind permission to reproduce their photographs:
Key: (t) top; (c) centre; (b) bottom; (l) left; (r) right
All images Dreamstime.com unless otherwise indicated.
4 (bl) Pascal Philp; 12–13 (c) iStock.com/banarfilardhi; 14 (br) LardoBalsamico,
22 (bc) MxcnKing926; 23 (tr) Jymlii Manzo; 24 (br) Colin Smith; 29 (tr) Zvijerka.